THE BENGAL CAT

Wouldn't it be a treat to own a small, friendly, affectionate domestic cat that looks very similar to one of the beautiful big cats at the zoo? Since the dawn of history, humankind has trapped or caught infant wild cats to keep as pets. The ancient Egyptians even used tamed, collared cheetahs to chase and bring down game for their own tables, much as modern falcons are used today. Painting on a thousand-year-old tomb wall depicts a small spotted cat helping a hunter kill waterfowl. But unlike dogs, large wild feline species never really accepted total domesticity. Only in recent years has a breed of domestic cat been developed to resemble the exquisitely spotted African leopard but in a tiny 13-pound package! These lovely little family pets are called Bengals and are charming the cat fancy and pet owners alike.

The Bengal is an exciting new breed of domestic cat that is not only dramatically beautiful but quite unique from other breeds of cats in its place within the family. They are alert, alive, and incredibly quick, making short work of anything small and moving such as bugs, mice, or toys. Cat show judges will testify to how startlingly fast a Bengal contestant can destroy a feather teaser. People who have owned cats from childhood report never

The allure of the Bengal cat comes in its exquisitely spotted coat and its affectionate, outgoing personality.

having owned a pet that they found as entertaining or enjoyed as much.

Of course, the first thing one finds enchanting is the strikingly beautiful leopard-like pattern of the thick, short fur. The unusually soft, light orange coat with its sharply contrasting dark spots is excitingly wild looking and new to the world of domestic cats. There have been other spotted breeds for many years, but none so feral in appearance and conformation while still being so dependably sweet natured. Technically a tabby patterned cat, Bengals are recognized in both the spotted and the classic (blotched or marbled) tabby patterns. In both varieties, vertical stripes on the body are undesirable.

In the spotted variety which is by far the most popular, the spots should be randomly spaced over the entire torso or aligned horizontally (never vertically). The size of the spots is not crucial, but larger ones are deemed preferable to smaller, and darker ones to lighter. Very dark spots against a light orange-tan or creamy ground color seem to attract the most attention. The spots themselves can vary. Some, like those of a cheetah, are similar to black ink splattered in droplets on a manila folder. But in the rarer types, the centers of those spots seem to

The desired coat pattern in the Bengal is technically a tabby pattern with dark spots most preferred.

have changed to a rusty brown color forming a spot called a rosette. Jaguars, leopards, and ocelots boast these beautiful variations. Rosetted Bengals are especially prized in a litter and can be very expensive to purchase. Sometimes rosettes

Shorthairs usually have only two colors mixed together in a vaguely bull's eye swirl, the marbled Bengal has several colors and shades, and there should be no circular motion to the shapes at all. Instead, a horizontal, flowing feel to the alignment is desirable.

Stripes, spots and rosettes give the Bengal its wild-cat look. This altered male is SGM A-Kerr's King Pin.

resemble a dark doughnut with a colorful center. Pawprint rosettes, formed by several little dark spots around a lighter central spot, are the rarest of all. Artificial fur fabrics often show the rosetted pattern in the most realistic coats and accessories.

The swirled or marbled pattern in Bengals is glorious to behold! Each kitten is unique in its areas of color. Whereas the common classic tabbies or American

The base color is the same as in spotted Bengals, i.e., the feet and nose coloration is similar in both types, usually a light cream or orangy color. The upper body, too, is usually made up of the same dark outlining, but around random shapes rather than around rusty spots. Some marbles have a great deal of black in the pattern, others are mostly a rich mahogany. But regardless, all should have at least three colors or shades: a light base color, a medium color forming the shapes, and a much darker outlining around each of the shapes. Some adults resemble stained glass with their dark outlining!

The popular leopard coloration is not the only accepted coloring, however. Just as there are white tigers, there are snow leopard Bengals. These can be either spotted or marbled in pattern, but instead of the warm colorful base coat, they have varying shades of ivory (as seen in Siamese,

Siamese cats do. Recently, however, the more valuable kittens have been born white but with the pattern quite visible from the start. All Bengals should show a well-defined pattern by the time they are four weeks old. While it is true that they darken with age, not only do the spots darken but so does the ground color. So if there is no contrast at weaning age, there probably never will be.

While kittens carry their tails high when happy, most adult Bengals hold their tails low, just

This two-week-old snow marble Bengal kitten exhibits the horizontal flowing feeling of the marble pattern as well as a lighter orangy coloration.

Tonkinese, and Burmese breeds). Some of these lovely cats have blue eyes, others green or yellow. Those with the most contrast between the base color and the color of the markings are the most eye-catching. There is as yet no "Dalmatian cat" for the ground color is never pure white. Some snow leopards are born almost white and develop the markings during kittenhood, just as

as wild cats do. Voices are seldom used in neutered adults except at dinner time. Kittens, on the other hand, can be insistent when lost, homesick, hungry, or needing the litter box. The timbre is often different than in other breeds of cats. An odd, raspy noise is unique to the Bengal.

Bengals vary in size, but most are about the same as an average barn cat. Because they are intended to be a toy-sized big cat, large Bengals are undesirable. Adult males sometimes reach 15 pounds, but appear heavier because they are long and muscular. They seem to be larger than they are, and should appear to be sturdy and substantial. Wispy, small-boned kittens will rarely develop into top quality cats.

It's easy to fall for the Bengal—here's two Bengal infants at seven days old showing impressive heads and the desirable small ears.

Heads should be formidable, but not rounded, domestic shaped faces. Noses should be heavy with a wide muzzle. Whiskers should extend from a pronounced pad, and the jaw should be pronounced, just as in the small, tree-dwelling jungle cats. Ears, too, should resemble most wild felines and be small and rounded.

PURRSONALITY

Extremely intelligent, Bengals are alert to anything new in the immediate environment and are curious to learn. This means that they get into things. When the groceries are brought into the home, the kitten insists on looking and sometimes going into the bag. It is virtually impossible to write a letter with a Bengal in the house without first letting it check out the moving pen. They follow their humans from room to room always to be near and sometimes upon the awaited lap. But before settling down for a snooze, they must first rub on the attached face, hair, neck, etc., while purring loudly. Some individuals are quite headstrong as to their likes and dislikes, much like any domestic cat and may prefer not to be picked up. They may squirm to get down, then jump into that same lap at their own discretion. Others prefer shoulders and all like heights. A tall carpeted cat tree with a soft privacy place on top will become the kitten's lifetime favorite spot. Or a thick pad atop the refrigerator or bookcase will do just as well.

Eager for human companionship and approval, this is a breed that can be taught the rules of the house (such as to stay off tables and kitchen sinks) with only a minimum of training. A sharp "No!", and a brush off the surface (or a bang on the tabletop with whatever is handy) will make the rule clear. Responding to kindness, they quickly observe what annoys their humans and will avoid the action. But by the same token, they must never be treated unkindly for they never forgive and trust again. Extremely sensitive, they become furtive and unapproachable if hit or hurt. Young children must be supervised until the kitten learns to stay just out of reach of small hands. As with any breed of cat, a Bengal will scratch if mistreated or teased. But they are dependable, predictable pets that do not lash out when unprovoked.

Bengals are natural retrievers of soft balls, crumpled bits of newspaper, or cat toys. With a little patience and some tempting treats, they can even be taught simple dog-like tricks such as sitting up, rolling over, or jumping over a fly swatter held horizontally. Then, if they are coaxed (and in the mood) they will perform for guests! Some become real show-offs, doing the tricks for visitors unasked.

No insult intended—the Bengal can be very dog-like in its outgoing personality and tendency to follow its owner around. This attentive Bengal is Topspot Asia sharing time with her owner Mary Magee.

Most Bengals enjoy water and will play for long periods in a bathroom sink with the faucet slightly running. They willingly get wet doing it, too! If a floating toy is dropped into a bathtub with a few inches of water in it, the cat's antics will delight children and adults alike, airlifting toy and

Like other cats, Bengals prefer affection on their own terms. Firefly has sought out his young keeper, Max McKee, for some quality time.

From a young age, Bengals' fixation with water is entrancing. This eight-week-old sea urchin is happily getting his feet wet.

water in all directions. Many Bengals will come right into a warm shower with their humans to "attack" the toes or play with the soap. It can be cute at the time, but a wet cat running about the house afterward is not so endearing! If allowed into the garden (under supervision, of course), Bengals will often play in the sprinkler or a running hose. Homes with swimming pools should attach a carpeted ramp in several places around the edge to avoid tragedy, just as one does when owning a dog. All cats can swim until exhausted, but other domestic breeds avoid pools. A Bengal kitten may try to bat at a floating leaf or bug and fall in. Curiosity may indeed kill the cat.

One of the questions often asked is, "Do Bengals get along

Around the pool, Topspot Asia and owner Charles Magee spend a wet summer afternoon. Although Bengals can swim—and may even enjoy it—they should never be allowed access to water without supervision.

with dogs and other breeds of cats?" In most cases, a purchaser would be introducing a tiny kitten into their home. It would probably be the smallest member of the family and would be properly respectful of its elders. It would grow up close friends with the entire family, providing the dog was willing. But, just as is the case with other domestic cats, adult Bengals are often reluctant to accept another adult cat and will need time to adjust to a

purring friend into their beds and will settle down to sleep cuddling the kitten rather than a teddy bear.

A Bengal is a wise choice for children with allergies, for the sleek, soft coat seems to hold many fewer allergens. It is a different type of fur; more like a pelt than ordinary cat fur, and sufferers of allergies claim that they can tolerate close facial contact with Bengals with fewer reactions. Many children can

Bengals are terrific choices for families with children, tending to seek out their family members. Mary Jean McKee has a special bond with Firefly.

newcomer in the home. With its quick intelligence, the Bengal may seek to dominate the newcomer, but after a few bouts of screaming at it, peace will again reign when dominance is established.

Bengals love attention and will welcome it from adults and children alike. Children have more time to play with the kitten and bond with it. They find enormous comfort in taking a

therefore sleep with a Bengal, which might not be possible with other breeds.

One word of warning here: Bengals are heavy cats and are fond of curling up to sleep in soft beds. Without realizing it, the cat can be too heavy for a baby under a blanket in a crib or bassinet and prevent the infant's breathing. All cats should be kept away from tiny children.

HISTORY OF THE BENGAL

The ancestry of the present-day Bengal cat is the most diverse of any breed in the world. It derives from a spotted domestic cat found in India, tabbies from several parts of California, and another species of feline called the Asian leopard cat (ALC). It is this beautiful little cat, often seen in zoos, that has made possible the unique appearance of its "manufactured" descendants.

Asian leopard cats are tiny spotted felines weighing about 10 underside. The entire cat is covered with dark spots or rosettes, much like their much larger cousins, the ocelot and the true African leopard. Care must be taken to refer to it as a leopard *cat*, not just as a leopard. There is about a 200-pound difference!

These spectacular little felines are shy and nocturnal. They eat mostly rodents and small birds, occasionally venturing into farm yards to prey on domestic chicks, much as raccoons do. Only one

The progenitor of the Bengal breed is the Asian leopard cat or *Felis bengalensis*, whence comes the name Bengal for the hybrid domestic breed we know so well.

pounds and indigenous to a large part of southern Asia. Technically called *Felis bengalensis*, the ALC has different sub-species that are found from southern India eastward through Thailand, Malaysia, and into China. The base coat as seen on the feet and face varies in color with different geological areas of origin. Most are of different shades of tan to orange, blending to a white sub-species is on the endangered species list; the other varieties are still quite plentiful in their native locales.

Assumed to be vicious by people who have never encountered one, ALCs instead are afraid of humans. For countless centuries they have been hunted with traps and spears. Only the most wary ones survived to reproduce in the wild, thereby continuing the shyest and most intelligent bloodlines. Most encounters with them by hunters were in traps or mother cats defending their young, when they of course can

A first-generation Bengal (50% domestic cat—50% Asian leopard cat) possesses the fabulous pelt of its wild forebears and some degree of domestication, though it is not as trusting as its future Bengal generation.

be most formidable and threatening. It is not in the nature of the tiny ALC to attack when unprovoked. They just want to be left alone. "Wild" does not mean vicious; but self-sufficient and untrusting of humans. We do not fear wild rabbits despite their sharp teeth and readiness to bite! ALCs, too, need not be feared if allowed their privacy. And their hybrid offspring are no more dangerous nor unpredictable than they are.

Until recently (with the CITES treaty to protect wild animals), natives throughout Southeast Asia used the pelts of these beautiful little cats to make handbags, shoes, hats, etc. for the fur trade. (ALC kittens are still seen for sale in native markets where they are considered to be a table delicacy!) It was this gloriously beautiful pelt that inspired early experimenters to attempt to hybridize them with ordinary tabby cats. The intent was to produce a friendly, dependable house pet with as many of the ALC's appearance characteristics as possible. A side advantage of such a striking little pet would be that people could legally own the new friendly variety and not be so eager to purchase wild kittens as pets, thereby reducing the illicit trade in live spotted wild cats. Worldwide, fashionable ladies might be less willing to wear leopard-skin

This Asian leopard cat exhibits well-defined rosettes that she will pass onto her progeny.

clothing if they owned a living, loving, toy leopard instead. There were many reasons and good intentions for attempting such a hybridization project.

There have been several such experimenters since the late

made further development impossible.

Subsequently several other people who owned ALCs produced hybrids, notably Pat Warren, William Engle, and Dr. Willard Centerwall working with Loyola

Natural mothers, Bengals can care for a fairly large litter with little or no help.

1800s, but credit is given to Jean Sugden for the first documented hybridization between *Felis bengalensis* and *Felis catus* in 1963. She used a solid black domestic tomcat. The resulting hybrid female, called Kiki, herself produced offspring, proving that a second generation was possible. But the line was discontinued in 1966 when a death in the family

University. The latter was investigating the components in the ALC immune system that seemed to give it a measure of immunity to feline leukemia. It was hoped that there could be some related significance to human leukemia research. Jean Sugden Mill, now remarried, obtained several of Dr. Centerwall's F_1 first-generation hybrid kittens and was able to continue her interrupted efforts to "put the gorgeous coat on a new, domestic breed of cat." Most of the Bengals in the world today trace back to those original Centerwall crossbreds.

But it took many years of disappointment and fruitless effort before it was determined that the males from these first generations were always sterile! Mules are sterile in both sexes, as are lion/tiger crossbreds. But

A swarming pile of Bengal newborns from Topspot cattery. Notice the fabulous markings and deep coloration on these very young kittens. Breeder, Barbara J. Andrews.

fortunately, ALC/domestic cat crosses are fertile in the female sex. It was then necessary to breed them to another, carefully chosen, friendly *domestic* tomcat, thereby diluting the wild inheritance by another half. Second-generation kittens were much less shy and were considerably more outgoing and friendly. Most of the males, too, proved after many trials also to be sterile.

The drama of the jungle seems captured in the deep blue eyes of this Bengal youngster.

A few second-generation kittens were exhibited in cat shows, the best known being Millwood Penny Ante, who drew enormous crowds wherever she was exhibited. She delighted cat lovers in Paris, Duzeldorf, and Toronto in 1985 as well as in cities all over USA, purring her way into the hearts of spectators and judges alike. People were enchanted, and men who had been dragged to the show by their wives would hover hybrids publicly in print and in the offices of cat registry associations and in State legislatures. Bengals found themselves vilified by people who had never even seen a Bengal, much less an Asian leopard cat. Humans always fear the unknown. Intensive education became, and still is, essential to reassure the public that Bengals are no more threat to their safety than any other domestic cat.

An eight-week-old litter looking convincingly wild and curious.

in front of the Bengal exhibit saying, "Now *there's* a cat I like!"

As might be expected, Penny Ante caused lots of controversy too. Purists were horrified at this "adulteration" of the wild species and opposed the concept itself. Breeders of other spotted breeds envisioned diminishing interest in their breeds when eclipsed by the wildcat's spectacular beauty, so attacked

In 1985, The International Cat Association (TICA) welcomed Penny Ante and other early kittens into their shows with exhibition-only status. Soon afterward, Bengals were permitted to compete in the New Breed and Color classes where they were handled by the judges. A standard was written to describe in detail the features to be rewarded in the show rings, and those to be penalized. The new breed had been born! Educational material was passed out to crowds of interested visitors at the huge cat shows sponsored by TICA, and the media gave the breed and the shows welcome publicity. It was not until 1992, however, that TICA admitted the breed into Championship status. Fourth-generation (or more) Bengals were now competing against all other breeds on an equal status! They looked, acted, and were accepted as domestic cats. A clear differentiation was made at this time between the first three generations and subsequent ones. Any Bengal with an ALC in a three-generation pedigree was considered to be a foundation

The first-generation males from the domestic cat—Asian leopard cat cross are sterile. This daring youngster is an F1 generation.

A five-week-old kitten bred by Pat Eib, camouflaging himself on a spotted carpet.

Bengal and not eligible to the show ring. This assured the fancy and the public that only well-bred Bengals carefully selected for sweet temperament would be competing at the shows. It also determined an arbitrary cut-off generation for designation as a "domestic" cat.

indicates a foundation Bengal, and the words "Not for Competition" are clearly typed on the registration by the TICA registrar. Bengals with an outcross to another breed of domestic cat in the first three generations also are considered foundation Bengals. Thus a cat

A six-week-old kitten, bred by Andrew De Prisco and Barbara J. Andrews, out of Topspot Simba and Geekers.

On registration papers, fourth generation and subsequent cats are identified by the letters SBT as the first digits in the cat's registration number. It stands for 'stud book.' Any other combination of letters or numbers

eligible for competition must be a purebred Bengal-to-Bengal offspring for at least four generations with nothing but Bengals on a three-generation pedigree. These are the kittens most people choose as pets.

CHOOSING YOUR BENGAL KITTEN

Prospective buyers of new kittens must give advance thought to various details before purchase. One should have a clear idea of the sex, color, markings, and quality preferred. Show-quality kittens will be quite expensive and should exhibit the characteristics desirable for the breed so that they have a distinct possibility of winning in a cat show. Any cat can be shown, but show quality means that it is destined to win a title. Somewhat less expensive are the breeder-quality kittens, which are of suitable quality to contribute desirable genes to their offspring to *improve* the breed. One does not need to actually breed them, but the quality is there to do so if desired. Pet-quality kittens are those sold as pets only, usually with papers held by the buyer until proof is given that the kitten has been spayed or altered. These are beautiful little Bengals, but have some fault that makes them unworthy of being bred or shown. It could be a slight fault along the tail or a vertical stripe over the rib cage, or ears somewhat too large, etc. Kittens with these faults or a white spot under the neck, or those of the wrong color make wonderful pets at a much lower price.

Spotted belly up and deep blue eyes...what a glorious feline creature! This three-week-old darling is out of Topspot Simba and Topspot Jafar.

Above: Topspot Simba represents a truly lovely Bengal female, and here she is cleaning her single kitten Liu. Below: Liu thanks mom for the licks and affection. Breeder, Andrew De Prisco.

Above and Below: Three-week-old Liu at her mom's nipple. Breeder, Andrew De Prisco.

Either sex makes ideal pets after neutering. Temperament is determined individually, and there is no reliable difference between the neutered sexes. But people have definite preferences based on previously owned cats. Males do tend to grow larger and deeper voiced.

Just as baby cheetahs are covered with an ugly coat of long gray hair at about the time of weaning, so, too, are most Bengal kittens. Called the "fuzzy uglies," this stage starts at about seven weeks of age and continues until about six months of age. Perhaps it is Nature's way of muting the bright coat, thereby protecting vulnerable kittens while they are still learning to care for themselves. Thus, a buyer is wise

At three days old, this female kitten shows the fuzzy coat that is typical of newborn Bengals.

to choose a kitten from a litter at about six weeks of age when they are still the color they will be at maturity. Of course, no kitten should leave home at that age, but a photo or drawing of the unique markings on the forehead will ensure the same kitten when

Notice the unique forehead markings on this kitten. Breeders use such markings to determine one kitten from another. On many Bengals, these markings are fairly distinct from birth.

adoption time arrives. After the fuzzy uglies have begun, buyers may deny that the preffered kitten is the same one chosen, and it is difficult to envision the beautiful animal that will emerge. A great deal of trust is needed between the buyer and seller. This is why a study of the parents is helpful in forecasting the adult appearance. Knowledge of the cats in the pedigree is helpful too.

show, then make appointments to visit the catteries at a later date. Of course you will call ahead before you arrive at a cattery. Never purchase a kitten from a breeder who will not let you view the kitten's quarters. You need to see the facility and at least the mother cat. Mama may be a little under the weather, yet nonetheless she still should embody a healthy and typy Bengal representative.

This healthy Millwood kitten shows a nice coat pattern coming through its partially fuzzy coat. You can be pretty certain this kitten will have what it takes.

By far, the best source for finding your Bengal is by word of mouth. Happy customers are always the surest harbingers of satisfaction. Probably the next best reference for a new kitten is an exhibitor at a cat show. There a prospective buyer can meet the many breeders with their Bengals on display, evaluate their animals, and review their literature. If there are no kittens being sold at the

Don't chance an unhealthy kitten. Be sure the cattery is kept clean and smelling good. It is hard to judge much about a Bengal kitten in the midst of the fuzzy ugly stage, so one needs all the clues possible.

Another possible source for finding a kitten is through the classified ads in either a local newspaper or a national cat magazine. Most breeders will send out promotional literature with colored photos upon request. Photos of the actual kittens available may be impossible to get because of the time involved. When the breeder finds several free hours to set up and shoot the snaps, processes the film, mails it out, waits for the payment, and arranges for shipment, the kitten is a couple weeks older and well may be sold already. No breeder can be expected to hold a kitten at weaning time while awaiting a possible long-distance sale based on photographs that never do the kitten justice. A wiser plan is to purchase the offered kitten with a seven-day return guarantee and mail payment immediately. Then if it is not as represented, it can be returned, costing only the air fare.

Purchasing kittens sight-unseen can be worrisome, of course, for there is something special about personally choosing a kitten from several nearly identical siblings. We all like to feel a little magic happens when a kitten chooses *us*. But most kittens are cute and cuddly and will win our hearts if given time.

Bengal kittens, however, come from a wide diversity of bloodlines and vary considerably even in the same litter. One needs a few guidelines to be certain that the

A certain amount of variation can be expected even within the same litter. This feisty gang of five bred by Andrew De Prisco and Barbara J. Andrews grew up to become some very handsome, well-marked Bengals. Owners, Doris De Prisco, Mary Magee and Jaime Gardner.

new kitten will be healthy, happy, and beautiful for its full lifetime.

Temperament is the primary consideration, for if the cat is untouchable, it is not a true pet. Bengal kittens display their natures as young as three weeks of age. If the kitten cowers in the corner of the nest box with lowered ears and a throaty growl, it will never become the child's companion that its more confident litter mates will become. Bengal babies should come forward to meet humans and purr contentedly when held. Most, however, will want to get down almost at once, for Bengals rarely like confinement, even in hands or arms. Most kittens are too busy exploring a visitor's shoes, shoulders, hair, and pant legs to sit still for long.

The true Bengal is a doll! The breed's temperament is that of the most people-oriented and outgoing of all felines. This doll is Betsy Thek's Nobell.

A new kitten should be taken to the veterinarian during the guarantee period to check for health problems such as heart murmur, leg joint irregularities, abnormally shaped rib cages, parasites, etc. Until the kitten has been vaccinated, it should be protected from any exposure to disease. This means guarding it against children's fingers poking into the carrier in the veterinarian's waiting room (the child may have just touched a sick kitty of his own). It means not allowing the doctor's attendant to hug it to her clothing (or even touching it without freshly scrubbed hands). And it means forbidding neighbors, friends, and visitors to touch or hold it if they own a cat (it could be a carrier of disease). Don't take it into public places or allow it to wander in areas where other cats may have walked (such as your back yard).

This four-week-old kitten from A-Kerr's Cattery is the future Ch. A-Kerr's Serendipity. Notice the lovely marble pattern developing.

New kittens should be watched carefully at first for signs of diarrhea or fever. Bengals sometimes are carrying microorganisms which lie dormant until the kitten is stressed by transfer from familiar surroundings. The kitten may eat well, play tirelessly, and seem normal, but if it feels light of weight or does not gain weight properly, the breeder should be consulted at once. *Giardia* is a common problem in Bengals.

During the first few days a new kitten should be confined to a small area, such as a porch or bathroom, until it has used its litterbox unerringly and knows where it is. Then it should be

Confine the newcomer to your home to just a couple rooms until he is comfortable. Within a few days, he should feel right at home.

permitted to wander further away gradually so that it maintains its bearings and can find its way back. Expecting a tiny kitten to locate a litterbox in a large home after being carried around is like setting a two-year-old child down in a museum and saying, "Find the bathroom." Most kittens playing in the living room will start to cry and wander around when they feel urgency. Alert humans will recognize the

Human handling makes the difference in rearing kittens, and Bengals should thrive on the attention of their human friends.

signal and help them to find the litterbox. Keep in mind that once a lost kitten "goes" behind the sofa, it may do so the rest of its life! The first two weeks are critical in establishing the correct habits.

Playing roughly with a baby Bengal is never advised. It may be cute to see it vainly bite a finger in mock anger, but it isn't cute when the kitten becomes a cat! Any kind of biting of humans should be prohibited right from the start. Substitute a toy or rope or slice of leather in the games. A surprise

snap with the fingers on the nose can effectively discourage biting. You must especially prohibit playful attacks on passing legs. A 15-pound cat velcroed to bare legs can break the skin even if the intent was playful mischief rather than serious harm. A companion cat or dog, however, can be a wonderful outlet for a Bengal's rompings and chasings. Two Bengal kittens will entertain themselves and the family as well!

Every Bengal should have at least one high perch of seclusion from the melee below. A tree covered by carpeting is ideal, for the cat can climb, jump, and sharpen its claws freely there. A well-loved tree becomes beautifully frayed over years of use. Another useful piece of cat furniture is an exercise wheel. Most Bengals will teach themselves to use it, but a little food or a feather teaser (or even a twig cut from a bush and stripped of all but the end leaves) will encourage the cat to walk on it in an effort to reach the treat.

LIVING WITH A BENGAL CAT

TRAINING YOUR BENGAL

Discipline is essential in training a cat, but it should never be done in anger. If a Bengal kitten is shown the rules of the house consistently while young, no discipline of an adult will be necessary. Every young kitten should be forced to lie upside down in the hands of its owner for very brief periods. No young kitten life. Even challenging, frightened kittens can be calmed with this method.

Shy, aloof kittens may change their attitudes if kept alone in a bathroom-sized area out of sight and earshot of all other animals and people for a few days. They will often become so lonely that they will welcome human attention after a while. They may then be allowed

Training a cat as alert as a Bengal is a delightful task (if you're patient and up for the challenge)! Owner, Tracy Smolo.

wants to do this for it exposes the vulnerable tummy. Thus if forced while the kitten is still very tiny (it's almost impossible to do this with a large cat), it learns that nothing dire happens and that it can trust the owner even when it is most helpless. Once this trust is established, the kitten will be easier to handle and train all its to mingle in the household.

Bengals are extremely bright and catch on to human requests quickly. They can learn to do tricks just as dogs do. Most are natural retrievers of soft items, but cats do not like to pick up hard objects with their teeth. With patience, they can be taught games of scent discrimination and to find hidden items or people. Those that are outgoing and fearless can be taught to walk on a leash in public or to ride on a shoulder. Kittens can be taught the stay command, but they have too much energy to obey it for very long periods. Humans must be fair in their demands, making training sessions short and fun.

CARE OF A BENGAL

Bengals need very little special care or grooming. The short coat needs only to be wiped off with a damp cloth during the spring and fall shedding season. Likewise, a close-toothed comb will take out loose fur and prevent hair balls and shedding onto the furniture. It is wise to keep the tips of the claws clipped flat with a guillotine-type clipper. This is easy if the kitten was taught to permit it while still tiny. Once clipped too short, causing pain, the cat may grow wary of having its claws clipped.

Food for a tiny weanling should be nutritious, well balanced, and soft. Gradually a high-quality dry food can be mixed with the soft in increasing amounts, until by four months of age, the kitten should be eating only dry food offered free choice. An empty plastic quart bottle with a head-sized hole in the side can be hung about a foot off the ground using a loop through its handle. A matching bottle for water beside it will keep a kitten or cat supplied over a long weekend without human attention. Unlike dogs, Bengals do not overeat unless very bored with nothing else to do. Given toys, a window to watch the birds, and loving people to lavish attention,

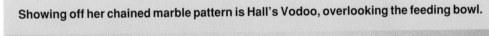

Showing off her chained marble pattern is Hall's Vodoo, overlooking the feeding bowl.

Bengals will maintain good health and a happy attitude without any special care.

All cats kept as pets should be neutered while still immature. The teeth should be cleaned and checked for unshed baby teeth simultaneously. Unaltered male cats are unsuited for indoor life. They become noisy as they mature and will usually begin to mark their territory with a pungent, foul-smelling urine. If neutered after maturity, a few individuals may no longer be offensive, but many will maintain the same unpleasant habits. These unfortunate cats are the ones that end up at the dog pound for euthanasia or are turned loose to starve unseen. A beautiful, loving male kitten deserves the security of being neutered before he becomes a nuisance. Most veterinarians urge the surgery before seven months of age.

Bengals, like all cats, prefer heights, giving them a good view over their territory. Be cautious about rowdy Bengals at the top of your staircase—many forget to stop and fall a floor or two! Owner, Sydney Martin.

An unaltered female is a no less annoying house pet. After maturity, she will make piercing cries on a three-week cycle. Heat periods last about seven days, during which she will not only "sing" but may use her sharp wits to escape the house and find herself a mate. It is virtually impossible to prevent her escape if there are children running in and out of the home. And if she is not mated, she may spray the walls just like a male does. Whole females can develop ovarian cysts from repeated cycles without pregnancy. The spaying operation is quite safe and is cheapest if done before maturity. It is quite expensive if done during the heat period or pregnancy.

MEDICATIONS

Bengals are domestic cats and are treated exactly the same as are other cats. They receive the same vaccination protection, the

Exercise for the Bengal makes the difference in musculature and tone. This Bengal gets his daily run on a wheel exerciser.

Bengals are playful and athletic. Indulge them with quality cat toys available from your local pet shop. Courtesy of the The Kong Company.

Many breeders utilize outdoor runs with nest boxes to give their Bengals necessary freedom, privacy, and the sense of the great outdoors.

An ideally situated cattery in a year-round warm climate. This is the new cattery at Millwood owned by the author.

same tests for disease, and the same treatments. The only significant difference reported is an increased tolerance for anesthetic, making it necessary for the veterinarian to administer the higher recommended dosage

especially on foundation generation Bengals.

In cases of severe diarrhea, metronidazole (flagyl) is the preferred medication, even when the veterinarian's fecal tests are negative.

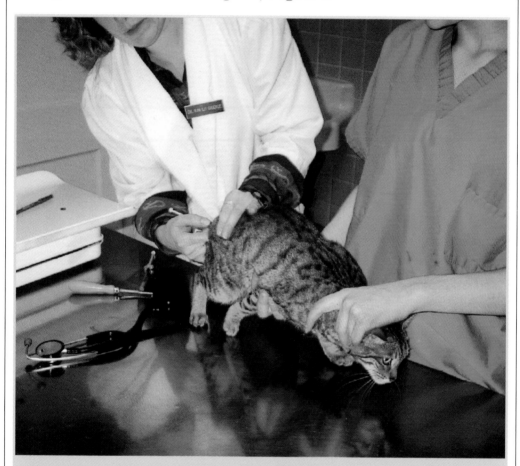

Bengals receive the same vaccinations as other domestic cats. Your veterinarian should know that Bengals tend to have a greater tolerance for anesthesia than do most other cats.

to obtain the same degree of anesthesia when neutering or performing other surgeries or procedures requiring sedation. Also, most veterinarians prefer to use killed-virus vaccines until the Bengal is four months old, rather than the modified live virus,

REGISTRATION

Each Bengal kitten should come with papers, including a record of vaccinations, a pedigree and a registration slip. The pedigree is a form which the breeder provides listing the kitten's family tree. It shows its parents, their parents, and their parents' parents. Some pedigrees go back even further. Each ancestor is named with its registration number and its color given. A certified pedigree may be purchased from the TICA office if not supplied with the kitten.

The registration application (blue slip) is an official document provided by the registration association showing the date of birth, sex, and that the parents were properly registered, were of the same breed, etc. It also shows the generation status and the number of brothers and sisters in the litter. If the kitten was purchased only as a pet, the breeder may insist upon holding the registration slip until the kitten has been neutered, thereby guaranteeing that it will not be used for breeding. Pet owners may not bother to send it in, for the blue slip has already assured the buyer of authenticity. Buyers of breeder- and show-quality kittens should expect to have all papers provided at the time of the purchase. The blue slip is then filled out with the name of the kitten and of its new owners and returned to TICA or other registry for the individual registration certificate. This certificate is necessary when showing or breeding the cat.

A record of any vaccinations or medications given to the kitten prior to sale should be included among the documents provided. This record should be taken with the kitten for its first visit to the veterinarian.

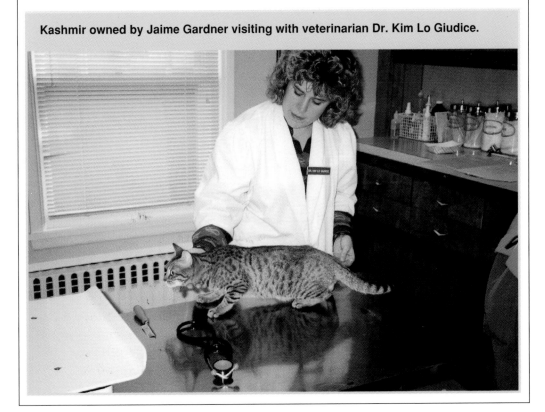

Kashmir owned by Jaime Gardner visiting with veterinarian Dr. Kim Lo Giudice.

THE STANDARD & COLORS

In order to determine the relative quality of a Bengal cat, or any other feline, there must be a standard against which the individual can be compared. The standards are prepared by a panel of experts within each cat registration body. Periodically these descriptive documents are amended to take account of progress within the breed, or to importance within the breed. Any person who has aspirations to exhibit, judge, or breed Bengals should have a knowledge of the standard. Only by constantly referring to it can a mental picture be developed of an outstanding Bengal.

To the beginner almost any Bengal would seem to be a fine example when they compare it to

A stunning marble pattern on the ten-month-old Ch. A-Kerr's Serendipity.

place more emphasis on a given aspect that may be regressing. The standard can never be precise, so is open to interpretation.

Within each standard, points are allocated to various features based on their believed the standard. The interpretation of the standard only becomes meaningful when combined with the experience of viewing poor, through mediocre, to those adjudged to be outstanding examples of the breed.

HEAD	10 POINTS
EARS	10 POINTS
EYES	5 POINTS
NECK	5 POINTS
BODY	10 POINTS
LEGS	5 POINTS
FEET	5 POINTS
COAT	10 POINTS
COLOR	10 POINTS
PATTERN	30 POINTS

RECOGNIZED CATEGORIES/ DIVISION/COLORS: Traditional Category, Tabby Division, Brown Spotted Tabby, Brown Marbled Tabby only. Sepia Category, Tabby Division, Seal Sepia Spotted Tabby, Seal Sepia Marbled Tabby only. Mink category, Tabby Division, Seal Mink Spotted Tabby, Seal Mink Marbled Tabby only. Pointed Category, Tabby Division, Seal Lynx Point (spotted or marbled) only.

GENERAL DESCRIPTION: The goal of the Bengal breeding program is to create a domestic cat which has physical features distinctive to the small forest dwelling wild cats, but with the loving, dependable, temperament of the domestic cat. Keeping this goal in mind, judges shall give special merit to those characteristics in the appearance of the Bengal which are distinct from those found in other domestic cat breeds.

All this talk of standards may be a little tiresome for this spotted beauty named Proclaim.

Tail—Thick. Medium large.

Feet—Large. Round.

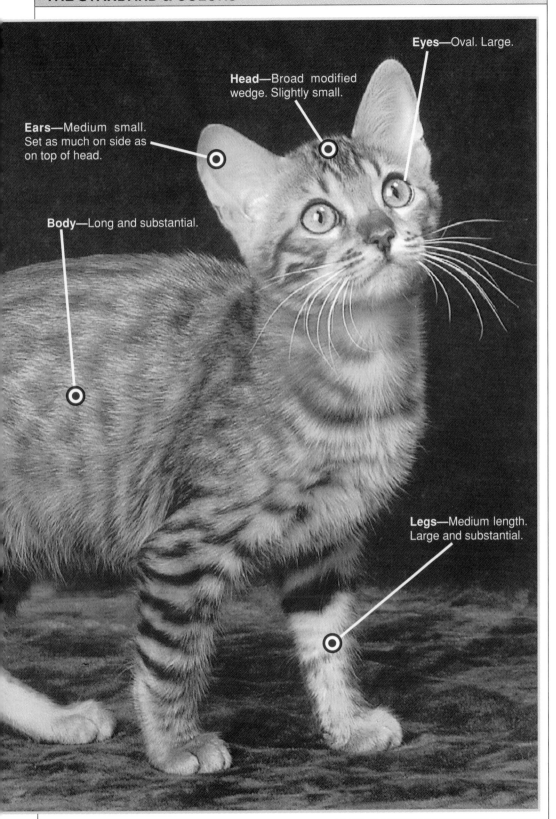

Eyes—Oval. Large.

Head—Broad modified wedge. Slightly small.

Ears—Medium small. Set as much on side as on top of head.

Body—Long and substantial.

Legs—Medium length. Large and substantial.

CONFORMATION: The conformation gives the Bengal cat a basic "feral" appearance. It is medium to large, sleek, and very muscular with hind-quarters slightly higher than shoulders. The head is a broad modified wedge with rounded contours, longer than it is wide, with a large nose and prominent whisker pads. The ears are medium set, medium small, short, with a wide base and rounded tips.

mascara markings desirable. Belly *must* be spotted.

The Marbled Pattern: Markings, while derived from the classic tabby gene, shall be uniquely different with as little "bull's-eye" similarity as possible. Pattern shall, instead, be random giving the impression of marble, preferably with a horizontal flow when the cat is stretched. Vertical striped mackerel influence is also undesirable. Preference should be

Serendipity shows off the rich color and glittery shine that distinguishes the Bengal coat.

PATTERNS

The Spotted Pattern: Spots shall be random, or aligned horizontally. Rosettes formed by a part-circle of spots around a distinctly redder center are preferable to single spotting, but not required. Contrast with ground color must be extreme, giving distinct pattern and sharp edges. Strong, bold chin strap and

given to cats with three or more shades; i.e., ground color, markings, and dark outlining of those markings. Contrast must be extreme, with distinct shapes and sharp edges. Belly *must* be spotted.

COLORS

Brown Tabby: All variations are allowed; however, a high degree of rufinism yielding a yellow, buff, tan, golden, or orange ground color is preferred. Markings may be virtually black, brown, tan, or various shades of chocolate or cinnamon. Light spectacles encircling the eyes and a virtually white ground color on the whisker pads, chin, chest, belly, and inner legs (in contrast to the ground color of the flanks and back) is desirable. Rims of the eyes, lips, and nose should be outlined with black, and center of nose should be brick red. Paw pads and tail tip *must* be black.

The ground color as well as the markings can vary from Bengal to Bengal: clear colors and sharp contrast are quintessential when assessing the Bengal's coat.

Seal Lynx Point: Ground color should be ivory to cream. Pattern can vary in color from dark seal brown, light brown, tan, or buff, with the light spectacles, whisker pads, and chin. There should be little difference between color of body markings and point color. Tail tip must be dark seal brown. Eye color: blue.

Seal Sepia Tabby/ Seal Mink Tabby: Ground color should be ivory, cream, or light tan with pattern clearly visible. Pattern may be various shades of sable brown to bitter chocolate. Ivory cream spectacles encircling the eyes, and ivory cream whisker pads and chin are desirable. There should be very little or no difference

The first marble Bengal at Millwood, bred by the author.

between the color of body markings and point color. Paw pads should be dark brown with rosy undertones allowed. Tail tip should be bitter chocolate (dark seal sepia/mink). Eyes may be gold, to green, to blue green.

TEMPERAMENT: Temperament must be unchallenging. Any sign of definite challenge shall disqualify. Cat may exhibit fear, seek to flee, or generally complain aloud, but may not threaten or harm. Bengals should be confident, alert, curious, and friendly cats.

PENALIZE: Spots on body running together vertically forming a mackerel tabby pattern, circular bulls-eye pattern on marbleds, substantially darker point (as compared to color of body markings) on Lynx Points,

Seal Sepia or Seal Mink. Any distinct locket on the neck, chest, abdomen or any other area not provided for in the standard. Do not penalize for mousy undercoat.

WITHHOLD ALL AWARDS: Belly not spotted. Paw pads not consistent with their color group description, or paw pads not all of the same color.

See Show Rules, ARTICLE SIXTEEN for rules governing penalties/disqualifications applying to all cats.

HEAD

Shape: Broad modified wedge with rounded contours. Longer than it is wide. Allowance to be made for jowls in adult males.

Size: Slightly small in proportion to body, but not to be taken to extreme.

The Bengal's body should be long and substantial, well muscled and medium to large in size. This is Ch. A-Kerr's Pick a Dilly.

Profile: Gently curving forehead to bridge. Bridge of nose extends above the eyes. Nose has a very slight concave curve.

Nose: Large and wide; slightly puffed nose leather.

Muzzle: Full and broad, with large, prominent whisker pads and high, pronounced cheekbones.

EYES

Shape: Oval, may be slightly almond shaped.

Size: Large, but not bugged.

Placement: Set wide apart, back into face, and on slight bias toward base of ear.

Color: Seal lynx point-blue. Seal sepia tabby or seal mink tabby-aqua (blue-green).

The Bengal's eyes should be oval or slightly almond shaped, and the ears should be medium small, set as much on the side as on the top of the broad, rounded head.

EARS

Size: Medium small, basically short ears, with wide base and rounded tips.

Placement: Set as much on side as top of head, following the contour of the face in the frontal view, and pointing forward in the profile view.

Furnishings: Light horizontal furnishings acceptable; but lynx tipping undesirable.

NECK

Size: Thick and muscular, large in proportion to head.

Length: Long, and in proportion to body.

BODY

Shape: Long and substantial, but not oriental or foreign.

Size: Medium to large (but not quite as large as the largest domestic breed).

Boning: Robust, never delicate.

Above left: **Close up of the marble pattern.** *Above right:* **Close up of the desired true black spots.**

Musculature: Very muscular, especially in the males, one of the most distinguishing features.

LEGS

Length: Medium, slightly longer in the back than in the front.

Boning: Large and substantial. Never delicate.

Musculature: Very muscular, like the body.

FEET

Size: Large.

Shape: Round.

TAIL

Shape: Thick, tapered at end with rounded tip.

Size: Medium large.

Length: Medium.

COAT

Length: Short to medium. Allowance for slightly longer coat in kittens.

Texture: Thick, luxurious, and usually soft to the touch.

COLORS

See Colors.

PATTERNS

See Patterns.

A-Kerr's Laser Light develops a beautiful rosetted coat. *Top:* Light (right) is playing with sibling at 11 weeks of age. *Middle:* Exploring at 16 weeks of age. *Bottom left:* Showing off rosettes at 12 months of age. *Bottom right*: All grown up and up a tree!

SHOWING YOUR BENGAL

Well-bred kittens between the ages of four and eight months are eligible to compete in any TICA show if the registration number starts with SBT. Several other cat associations now welcome Bengals to their shows as well. Check with the entry clerk before entering. To locate a show in a specific city or area, note the listings in the cat magazines. You may also telephone a breeder in the area who plans to attend. If months old. Adults compete for championship awards and points, just as all the other breeds do. In the judges' finals, in which each judge chooses his or her best ten cats in the show, Bengals compete against all the other breed winners directly. Of course, temperament is judged too, and only sweet-natured, calm cats should be exhibited. Visitors to the show are always delighted with the Bengal classes and love

At a cat show, the alertness and temperament of a competing cat are assessed by the judge. Bengals are enthusiastic, winning contestants!

there are no TICA shows listed in your area, you may want to consider starting an affiliated club that accepts Bengals.

To be eligible to show, adult Bengals must have an individual registration number starting with the letters SBT and be over eight to watch them playing enthusiastically on the judging stands. Visit a cat show to learn the procedure and equipment needed before entering your Bengal. Altered cats may be shown in the alter class and win premiership awards.

ABOVE: Here's Millwood Baffle being examined by the famous cat judge and geneticist Dr. Solveig Pflueger. Owner, Jean S. Mill.

BELOW: Show cats must be amenable to being handled by strangers. This leopard-clad judge is carefully examining her similarly spotted participant.

All-breed judge John Burch examines a lovely Bengal at a cat show.

Note the relaxed disposition of this Bengal being reviewed by the judge.

New and potential Bengal owners are encouraged to attend cat shows in their area to meet the people who are actively campaigning and breeding Bengals. Cat shows are less formal and more fun than dog shows, and you will have the opportunity to chat with exhibitors and judges alike.

Provided on an occasional basis, wisely selected treats add variety to the diet and act as a cleansing agent against tartar buildup. Courtesy of Heinz.

Show cats just like pet cats need regular grooming. Brushes and nail clippers available from pet shops are recommended. Courtesy of Four Paws.

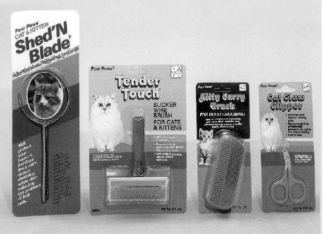

BENGAL BREEDING

Beautiful well-bred Bengals that are worthy of passing along their genes to a new generation to *improve* the breed are considered to be breeder-quality. Owners must give a great deal of thought to all that is involved in wanting kittens. Just as it requires responsibility to bring baby humans into the world, so too with feline babies.

time and energy, and a strong emotional makeup in the face of disappointment and tragedy, then the Bengal breed is a wise choice. Strong, reproductively healthy, and close to Nature's voice, these cats breed willingly, giving litters of from two to seven kittens. Mothers are responsible caregivers and have ample milk. They know just what to do

Breeders must know that every kitten produced has a home before a breeding is undertaken. This promising litter was bred by Dan Fairbanks.

Owners should have a clear idea of what is to become of any kittens they produce and be certain beforehand that there is a ready local market for their pets. There are already a great many baby Bengals being born every year, and one does not want to further burden the animal rescue organizations with unwanted kittens, no matter how lovely each one is. However, if a new breeder has proper facilities, sufficient

unassisted. In fact, owners are well advised to stay well away from pregnant queens during birthing so as not to distract the mother from her instinctive ritual.

Because Bengals have inherited a fresh dose of health and instinct genes from their not-so-distant wild ancestors, they are usually better equipped to reproduce than many of the long-established pure breeds of cat. Remember that many of the males in the

ABOVE: A three-week-old Bengal can be an armful for her attentive mother. Simba and baby Liu owned by Andrew De Prisco.

BELOW: At approximately six weeks of age, these four Bengal siblings represent an average litter size for the breed. Litter size ranges from two to seven kittens.

foundation generations are sterile or nearly so. It rarely pays to rear or maintain a foundation-generation male for breeding despite its beauty.

Quarters for keeping a mature stud Bengal should be outdoors if weather permits in a large run with sunshine and space for exercise. It should have high shelves for sunning and a high shady area as well. He needs an enclosed area that is warm, dry, and out of the wind for his bed and food during inclement weather. He will probably spray the walls of his quarters and may even wet on his bed, so everything must be easily cleaned. His food and water containers must be hung higher than his hips so that he cannot spray into them. Bengal tomcats can be very noisy, especially in the spring and summer, so he must be distanced from neighbors. Otherwise, it may be necessary to have his vocal chords clipped to bring his voice to a whisper—though this is not ideal.

No cat should be allowed to run freely outdoors, but especially not breeding animals. A queen will become pregnant even before her owner notices that she is in season. Unlike in dogs, there is no visual indication of approaching heat, and if she has access to a neighbor male, she may never call nor show any signs at all. Whole

At eight months of age, this is Julie from Furrari Bengals owned by Roz Wheelock. Julie is out of Jean Leonard's Tigger.

Bengals should never be allowed to roam outdoors. Even though your Bengal may be perfectly content stalking an unexpecting starling, you, your cat, and the neighborhood bird population are better off if your Bengal is behind closed doors.

males allowed to roam will become a nuisance to the neighborhood with their piercing screams of challenge to other males and their spraying on cars, windows, etc. They will meet with cruel fates or get into bloody nightly combats with other toms. Not to mention, too often beautiful Bengals are stolen when allowed to wander unsupervised.

Most owners of breeding females do not have suitable facilities to maintain a whole male tomcat and instead must elect to send their queens away for stud service. This is wise for the queen can then produce litters by a variety of males over the years, rather than repeatedly by the same in-house stud. Some breeders find, however, that a few Bengals, especially the foundation-generation females, form lasting preferences for certain males and may not accept any other males during their lifetimes!

SBT females usually are relaxed when visiting the male and accept his advances after a few hours of courtship. Once mated, the queen will permit repeated matings over a period of about three days. It is well to send a virgin queen to an experienced tomcat who will pursue her patiently but will not accept "No" for an answer. He will know the endearing voice that will win her over and will mount the most challenging of females undeterred. Young males may be cowed by an unwilling queen and not dare to approach her. Owners must watch inexperienced tomcats, too, lest they misunderstand the queen's screeches and attack her afterwards.

Pregnancy lasts about 63 days in Bengals. The queen will begin to eat more and will become quite affectionate to humans and other cats. An experienced breeder will be able to detect an increase in girth at about five weeks. A queen carrying only one kitten may conceal her condition completely and surprise her unsuspecting family on the appointed day.

About two weeks before delivery, a nest box should be put into her cage or run. If she is an

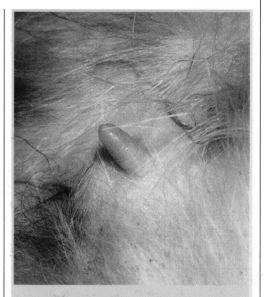

The pregnant queen's teats will become pronounced and the surrounding fur will clear to make them easily detectable by hungry sucklers.

For the first few weeks of a kitten's existence, mom is responsible for stimulating excretion.

Kittens instinctively find an available teat on which to nurse. Breeders often clip the kitten's very sharp claws so as not to injure the queen.

indoor cat, several nest boxes should be placed around the birthing room, one on the floor in a corner, one on a table, and perhaps another on top of something high. The box can be as simple as a carrying kennel with the door removed and a towel draped over the top to keep drafts out of the louvers. A clean, roomy pasteboard box is also suitable with a large hole at one end and several small air holes in the sides and back. The entry hole should be cut in the upper half of the box so that kittens cannot be dragged

A single kitten has no competition for her mom's teat. Nature shuts down mom's other "faucets," leaving only one or two for the single kitten to nurse from.

outside when attached to nipples. A carpet scrap cut to the exact size of the floor of the box works well as a base under the bedding. Using a large needle and heavy thread, secure the corners of the carpet down in the corners because Bengal mothers are strong cats and will attempt to

of innate instinct for birthing safely. They rarely need human monitoring or help. If allowed privacy and quiet without the distraction of a hovering family, they will deliver a healthy litter unaided. Bengals make loving, caring mothers and will stay curled up with their babies

Kittens should be weaned from their mothers by six weeks. If permitted, kittens will nurse from their mothers past three months. Here the very tolerant Bali is pictured with her twelve-week-old Patticake and Calipurr owned by Pat Eib.

make a nest depression in the bedding. Bedding should be lots of small pieces of cloth, not an entire towel, for kittens can be caught in the folds and smothered. Shredded newspaper is suitable too. The nest boxes should face away from the center of the room for privacy and be well secured against falling.

Bengal queens have a great deal

sometimes for several days before venturing out to eat and potty. By putting the mother in another room, one can then inspect the brood without worrying her unduly. Do not attempt to clean or change the bedding until the kittens are at least two weeks old, for the birthing odor is important to the new litter. The nest box should be lowered to the floor before the kittens can climb out (three or four weeks of age).

Once the sex and color pattern has been recorded for each kitten, a litter application form should be completed and sent to the registry association with the required fee. A pedigree should also be made out for each kitten. This will ensure that the necessary papers will be available to the buyers of the kittens at the time of sale.

Unless you have experience, sex can be difficult to determine in newborn kittens. The presence of a tiny vertical slit just under the anus identifies the females. Males are everything else, for they can vary somewhat in appearance when tiny.

Baby kittens need nothing except their mother for the first six weeks of age. It is usually a mistake to attempt to wean them

This two-and-a-half-week old is Kodiak, a seal sepia spotted male.

any earlier unless the litter is huge in number. Never feed weanling kittens cow's milk in any form (they cannot easily digest it), nor jars of baby meat with powdered onion listed as one of the ingredients. All meat should be cooked slightly to kill bacteria, especially hamburger. A premium

Young kittens can be introduced to solid foods gradually, and most will take to it with a little encouragement.

dry cat food (growth formula) can be pureed with cooked chicken in a blender and mixed with a wet canned cat food for the early weaning efforts. A little bit placed on the roof of the mouth can tempt the baby to eat. Bengal kittens are somewhat slower to wean themselves than some other breeds. When they are ready, the mother cat will hang back from the dish to allow them to eat first. She will also teach them to use the litterbox, but they should have a low-sided one at first that is easily entered. Baby kittens should be confined to a small area around the nest box so that they can easily find the litterbox, water bucket, etc. They must not be allowed to mingle with other household pets until they are well vaccinated at about nine weeks of age. The veterinarian should examine each kitten for any genetic faults such as heart murmur, tail fault, rib irregularity, etc.

It is wise not to take the kittens all away from the mother cat at the same time. She may grieve and suffer from breast discomfort. Despite what empathetic owners claim, she will not notice the disappearance of one or two kittens from a larger litter unless they cry as they are being carried away. If carried by the nape of the neck, they will remain docile and silent until out of earshot.

These three Bengal kittens show off their lynx and seal mink coats.

Liu, bred by Andrew De Prisco, shows off her dynamic dark markings, broad skull and ideally placed little ears.

Bengal kittens are curious explorers like most cats—this Big Girl has seated herself comfortably in her feeder.

THE FUTURE OF THE BENGAL BREED

It is difficult to fully convey the delight of owning a Bengal cat! They are so intelligent and responsive that they become adored family members almost at once. The beauty is what first attracts cat lovers to the breed, but it is the personality that makes them enthusiasts!

The Bengal breed is still evolving and improving

The International Bengal Cat Society (TIBCS) has members all over the world who are helping to further the cause and educate the public. It publishes a quarterly newsletter with pictures, articles, and a listing of reputable breeders worldwide.

In the years to come, top-quality Bengal kittens will have the beautiful rosettes, white

This beauty all grown up is Liu, owned by Lori and Mike Krikorian, an adored member of the family.

dramatically each year. It has now become recognizable from the other spotted breeds by its distinctive markings, color, and characteristics. But no Bengal has ever reached the goal as stated in the standard.

tummies, tiny ears, rich colors, and soft coats that resemble their wild ancestors. But they will maintain the sweet, loving, dependable temperament that makes them so endearing as family companions.

No matter how perfect and eye-catching are the spots and stripes of the Bengal, the breed's true uniqueness lies in its sweet, dependable nature. Here Firefly is being hugged by Mary Jean McKee.

KEEPING YOUR BENGAL HEALTHY

VACCINATIONS

There are a few extremely dangerous diseases that afflict cats, but fortunately there are vaccines that can dramatically reduce the risk of them infecting your Bengal. The bacteria and viruses that cause such diseases are often found in the air wherever there are cats. Discuss a program of immunization with your vet.

When a kitten is born, it inherits protection from disease thereafter each year. Potential breeding females should be given boosters about three to four weeks prior to the due date. This will ensure that a high level of antibodies is passed to the kittens.

An important consideration with regard to the major killer diseases in cats is the treatment of infection. If a cat survives an infection, it will probably be a carrier of the disease and shed the pathogens continually

Newborn kittens inherit protection from their mother's milk, thus the health of the mother will indicate the vitality of her offspring. Breeder, Barbara J. Andrews.

via the colostrum of its mother's milk. Such protection may last for up to 16 weeks—but it varies from kitten to kitten and may last only six weeks. It is therefore recommended that your kitten be vaccinated against diseases at six to eight weeks of age just to be on the safe side. Boosters are required some weeks later and throughout its life. The only safe course is therefore to ensure that your kittens are protected. The main diseases for which there are vaccinations are as follows:

Rabies: This is a disease of the neurological system. It is non-existent in Great Britain, Ireland, Australia, New Zealand, Hawaii, certain oceanic islands, Holland,

Sweden, and Norway. In these countries, extremely rigid quarantine laws are applied to ensure it stays that way. You cannot have your cat vaccinated against rabies if you live in one of these countries, unless you are about to emigrate with your cat. In all other countries, rabies vaccinations are either compulsory or strongly advised. They are given when the kitten is three or more months of age.

Feline panleukopenia: Also known as feline infectious enteritis, and feline distemper. This is a highly contagious viral disease. Vaccinations are given when the kitten is about eight weeks old, and a booster is given four weeks later. In high-risk areas, a third injection may be advised four weeks after the second one.

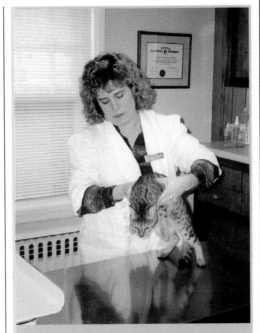

Your Bengal must be vaccinated against rabies and other feline diseases. Your veterinarian will be able to advise you of a responsible inoculation schedule. Owner, Jaime Gardner.

For the health of your family and your Bengal cat, responsible health care including proper precautionary measures is essential.

Feline respiratory disease complex: Often referred to as cat flu but this is incorrect. Although a number of diseases are within this group, two of them are especially dangerous. They are feline viral rhinotracheitis (FVR) and feline calicivirus (FCV). The vaccination for the prevention of these diseases is combined and given when the kitten is six or more weeks of age; a booster follows three to four weeks later.

The disease is easily spread via the saliva of a cat as it licks other cats. It is also spread prenatally from an infected queen to her offspring via the blood, or when washing her kittens. This is why it is important to test all breeding cats for FeLV. Vaccination is worthwhile only on a kitten or cat that has tested negative. If a cat tests positive for the disease, it has a 70 percent chance of survival, though it will be a carrier in many instances.

A friendly Bengal kitten can become a welcome addition to the household that already has an adult cat. Remember that every cat in your home must be properly vaccinated, since many feline diseases can be passed from one to cat to another.

Feline leukemia virus complex (FeLV): This disease was first recognized in 1964, and a vaccine became available in the US in about 1985. Like "cat flu," the name is misleading, because it is far more complex than a blood cancer, which is what its name implies. Essentially, it destroys the cat' s immune system, so the cat may contract any of the major diseases.

Feline infectious peritonitis (FIP): This disease has various effects on the body's metabolism. There are no satisfactory tests for it, but intranasal liquid vaccinations via a dropper greatly reduce the potential for it to develop in the tissues of the nose.

PARASITES

Parasites are organisms that live on or in a host. They feed

Showing off his swatty stuff is Topspot Jazzman at eight weeks old. Jazzman is a housecat who has an absolutely ideal temperament, completely loving and attentive to his owner Andrew De Prisco.

Blessed with the voice of an angel, this is Sheena, the Bengal who enlivens the multi-cat household of Doris and Louie De Prisco. Sheena lives with a Himalayan (Samson) and two regular cats (Pumpkin and Boots).

from it without providing any benefit in return. External parasites include fleas, lice, ticks, flies, and any other creature that bites the skin of the cat. Internal parasites include all pathogens, but the term is more commonly applied to worms in their various forms.

All cats are host to a range of worm species. If worms multiply in the cat, they adversely affect its health. They will cause loss of appetite, wasting, and a steady deterioration in health. At a high level of infestation, they may be seen in the fecal matter, but normally it will require fecal

Another thousand good reasons to keep your cat indoors is demonstrated by the beautiful Ch. A-Kerr's Pick a Dilly: hundreds and hundreds of ticks, fleas, and other buggy intruders threaten her in the grass.

External parasites and their eggs can be seen with the naked eye. All can be eradicated with treatment from your vet. However, initial treatment will need to be followed by further treatments because most compounds are ineffective on the eggs. The repeat treatments kill the larvae as they hatch. It is also important that all bedding be treated or destroyed because this is often where parasites prefer to live when not on the host.

microscopy by your vet. This will establish the species and the relative density of the eggs, thus the level of infestation.

Treatment is normally via tablets, but liquids are also available. Because worms are so common, the best husbandry technique is to routinely treat breeding cats for worms prior to their being bred, then for the queen and her kittens to be treated periodically. Discuss a testing and treatment program with your vet.